Winds of Change

The Poetry of
Gary A. Rosenberg

The Book Couple
Boca Raton, FL

Published by:

The Book Couple, LLC
21161 Via Ventura
Boca Raton, FL 33433
www.thebookcouple.com

ISBN: 978-0-9908458-4-3

Cover and interior by Gary A. Rosenberg

Printed in the United States of America

Contents

To my wife, Carol,
who rescued me from my misery;
to my son, Justin,
who gave me a sense of continuity;
to all my friends who stood by me;
and—of course—to my loving family

Poems of the Heart

Ode to a Working Woman

A tired maiden sleeps beside me
lost in the rhythm of the train.
Her face bears a smile, betraying her dreams
To see her makes me happy again.

Her perfume is sweet, though late in the day;
her blush is soft and paled.
Blond hair rests about her face,
Leaving it partially veiled.

Ah, sleeping beauty, open your eyes
that I may look into them!
   Two crystal beads that sparkle with life,
      and I can see right through them.

         But on she sleeps, oblivious
            of my tender emotion.
            If she'd but wake I'd be hers for life
            and pledge my undying devotion.

               Yet, this is just a fantasy
                  one that could never come true;
                  Unless she wakes, and
                     turning to me
                        says, "I was dreaming
                           of you!"

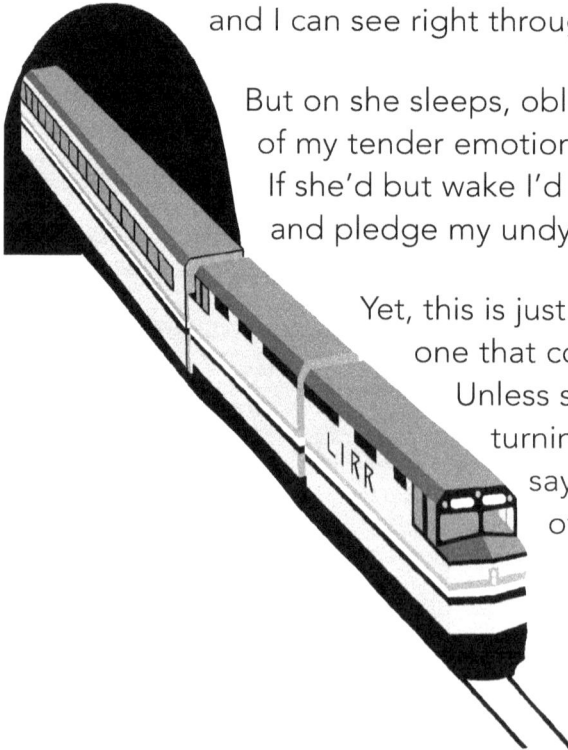

Dream, Come True

Last night I dreamt I was making love to the loveliest woman
  in the world.
Her skin was soft, her eyes were deep, her hair was blond and curled.
She held me with such passion, her arms embraced me tight.
I tenderly kissed her face, her neck–the moment seemed so right.
Slowly I undressed her, as she was helping me;
I saw her in the moonlight–beautiful was she!
I ran my fingers slowly from her neck down to her waist;
Her perfume in my nostrils was a fragrance I could taste.
Then I kissed those lips of red; my body was afire.
She responded enthusiastically, and drove me even higher.
My roving hands did then explore her secrets down below.
As they became familiar, I felt desire grow.
I longed to be as one with her, to join in ultimate bliss;
To be together always in an everlasting kiss.
Then we were inseparable–our bodies moved as one;
As we neared our climax, the mood was not undone.
Simultaneous explosions shook us to the heart:
Reverberating infinities of which we were a part
Seemed to draw in around us and hold us in their grasp;
A galaxy of wonder that instantly made us gasp.
We'd been to the ends of the universe and back again, she and I;
An experience so moving I wanted just to cry.
So I looked into her eyes and immediately was lost
Within the wild beauty of crystal, tempest-tossed.
I told her that I loved her then, and she replied the same
(The chaos deep inside us placated now and tame.)
My mind was thinking clearer, my feelings were so strong
I knew for sure what we had done was anything but wrong.
And once again I felt desire–her love I longed to take.
But she said, "Better still, darling, wait till you're awake."

Anniversary Rhyme

I can send you flowers to show my
  love
But they would just wither and fade.
I could shower you with expensive
  gifts
The finest things ever made.

But the most precious gift can scarce
  be bought
nor seen, nor touched, nor held.
A present to last eternity
That can't by death be felled.

The gift I give you is my love.
(I hope you don't think me vain!)
I want to share my hopes and dreams
And relish in all we gain.

But the heart is such a fragile thing
As tenuous as life itself.
To open up to someone else
can be dangerous to one's health.

Sometimes, though, when love is
  true
The hearts that share grow strong.
Two people find their lives are
  joined
By a thread that's sure and long.

But we can't ignore our problems
(As blind as love can be)
To keep the bonds between us
  secure
Sometimes we must disagree.

Lovers will quarrel, friends can fight
When they don't see eye to eye.
Sure we've had our share of those,
They'll continue as life goes by.

But we'll always rise above such
  things
Our hearts will pull us through.
Our feelings for each other are so
  intense
And our love so powerful and true.

You are the other half of my heart
Filling the void in my life.
A partner to last me all my days—
A lover, a friend, a wife.

So on this day we celebrate
The anniversary of our legal vow.
But our real joining came lives
  before
We commemorate that now.

I remember that my whole life
  through
Great anticipation was always there:
On the edge of some great discovery
That would come from I knew not
  where.

I did not quite feel empty
Though I knew I was far from full.
And the first time that I saw you
I felt fate renew its pull.

Pulling our lives together,
Pushing two hearts into one.
Causing a love to take to wings;
That has only just begun.

Though our journey is just started
We seem to be picking up speed.
The love we have between us
Is all the fuel we need.

We'll soar to distant galaxies
Powered by sheer emotion,
With mutual feelings reaching out
Of love and dear devotion.

I feel that I know you very well,
And I think that you know me, too.
But as much as we have experienced,
There's so much more we will go
    through.

I look forward to those times to
    come
The memories we'll save and
    share.
To spend my years without you
Is something I couldn't bear.

So stay beside me always
And I'll stand by your side.
Hold on tight with open eyes
As we continue our life-long ride.

And as each cherished year goes by
We'll surely thank God above,
For permitting us to join in life–
And in everlasting love.

Never will my thoughts for you
cease to grow in intensity.
My words seem inadequate to
    describe
A thing of such immensity.

How much I appreciate the things
    you do
I could tell you a million times,
How strong my feelings are for you
I reiterate in metered rhyme.

Yet even the most passionate poetry
Could surely not convey
Just how much in love with you
I'm falling every day.

And how my song for you is done
But only on this page.
The song for you that's in my heart
Will never die nor age.

For though our bodies grow feeble
And remembering things gets
    tough,
Just having you beside me
Will always be enough!

My Forever Valentine

Here's a special Valentine's poem
   written just for you.
It's the very romantic story
   of a love that's oh so true.
A lonely boy once happened to meet
   A girl who had given up on men.
He seemed so very eager
   That she thought she'd try again.

Now, he was not like all the rest,
And neither, in fact, was she.
She told him he was handsome;
He replied that she was
lovely!
She was kind and caring and warm
They shared such wonderful times:
Words of love flowed back and forth
Spoken, and in rhymes.

They shared a very special love,
   One so very rare.
They promised to stay united
   And for all time to care.
This couple's still together,
   They'll outlast eternity.
If you haven't already guessed,
   This couple is you and me!

Blossom in Blond

A woman came to the lonely meadow to walk amongst
   the flowers.
She picked a few, held them in her hand–they brought
   her a moment of joy.
Yet in gathering them to appreciate their life,
   she lost that most valuable quality.
Eventually, disheartened, a look of pain and loss on
   her face,
she let them fall to the ground.
It seemed a piece of her had died along with each
   wilted daisy.
So on she wandered.
I was as if a flower in that meadow, growing wildly.
She noticed the way my strong stem supported the
   blooming flower atop,
how broad leaves spread at my sides to absorb the light.
Roots stretched firmly into the moist soil, bringing me
   nutrients and support.
As she grew nearer, I feared she would trample me,
   or pull me carelessly from the earth.
Yet she did neither.
Slowly, she leaned over to smell the fragrance
   of my delicate blossom.
She sighed softly, and gently touched
   my quivering leaves.
Her touch was as soft and as warm as
   the sunlight–it made me happy.
It was then that I noticed that
   throughout the entire meadow
there was no flower that was more
   beautiful than she.

To Mom and Dad:

It's very rare to find these days
the magic you both possess.
How long you will go on for
is anybody's guess.
Who would have thought, way back then,
so many years ago
that the love you found when you were young
would flourish and continue to grow?
Very often couples find the love they had is lost.
And like a ship upon the sea their love becomes
storm-tossed.
Mighty breakers rock once steady boats,
they keel to starboard and port.
The ones who survive the furies of life
are a very special sort.
They're able to give when there's nothing left,
always ready to share,
To stand beside each other
and forever show they care.
Through the good and bad, the highs and lows
life's journey is often unsteady;
But love can help us persevere
and keep us on the ready.
Ready to appreciate
what living has in store,
So we can enjoy life while we're here
before there is no more.
Gloria and Henry, mom and dad,
show us how you've done it.
If life's a game, as some will say,
then you have surely won it.
A lovely home, a healthy life,
fine friends and family;
Who gather round at special times
and chorus merrily:
Happiness, joy, marital bliss;
a relationship of perfection.
A powerful love between two folks
that gives our lives direction.
So let us now express our thanks
for all they've brought to be;
and look with hope towards the future
with Gloria and Henry.

I Didn't...

I didn't buy my love a rose—
she said it was okay.
I didn't have to buy her things,
she loved me anyway.

I didn't buy my love a gift—
I thought she wouldn't mind.
She said I gave her many things,
and always treated her kind.

I didn't buy my love a ring—
I didn't see the point.
She just sadly hung her head,
and seemed all out of joint.

I didn't sing my love a song,
I didn't write her a poem,
I didn't buy my love a rose—
and now she has left home.

Miss Taken for Granted

I took my beloved for granted
Thinking she would always be mine.
For she had become so familiar
That I didn't give her quality time.

When we first fell in love I adored her
and would do anything she might
    ask.
But soon my attentions did dwindle
Our relationship became as a task.

One day I carelessly forsook her;
Forgot her as though an old shoe.
And though it was not my intention,
to my beloved I was untrue.

At first she could not believe it,
Her lover leave her behind?
She questioned my motivations
And me, I paid her no mind.

She probed deeper then for an
    answer—
an answer that I would not give.
With a man so cold and uncaring
she told me she just couldn't live.

I let her walk out of my life then;
I've regretted that day ever since.
For she was so like a princess
and she thought of me as her
    prince.

She would have done anything
    for me,
I was so blind I just didn't care.
How could I have been so stupid?
Why had I been so unfair?

So I decided that I would go seek
    her
though long and hard be the
    search.
For her I would look forever,
and seek to the ends of the earth.

But when my journey was ended,
and failure was all that I knew,
She came to me in my tortured
    dreams
And told me it just wasn't true.

She said she had always loved me;
and that she did love me still.
Our love was a force so powerful
that thoughtlessness couldn't kill.

I told her my love was undying,
and promised to join her real soon.
She looked away rather sadly,
singing a dirgeful tune:

"My beloved was the man I had
    dreamed of
He made all his secrets ours.

I shared with him all sorts of
  pleasures
like music and laughter and
  flowers.

"I thought to be with him forever,
yet forever's just as long as it lasts.
And like music and laughter and
  flowers
these things just became pleasant
  pasts.

"Then they were all but forgotten,
as I thought you'd forgotten me.
With my hopes and dreams rudely
  shattered
I walked on into the sea.

"I let the waves crash around me,
I felt that my death would be sooth.
But with my last bit of
  consciousness,
I realized the ultimate truth:

"Though we may take one another
  for granted,
and the things we feel we won't say,
We don't try as hard as we used to,
Love seems to just fade away.

"But life is too short for such folly,
we live, some love, all die.
We must hold on to those we
  treasure,"
she said with a tear in her eye.

"I must go now, my beloved,
but remember these words that
  I say:
Be true to yourself and your loved
  ones
until your dying day.

"And when that day is upon you,
look back at your life and smile.
For you will know for certain
that you loved me all the while.

After the First

I did not ask you into my life to cause you pain or grief.
And yet, as surely and inevitably as death itself, I will hurt you.
Like death, it is something I try at all costs to avoid.
As we grow to know one another, in all states of mind,
   in all situations that life throws at us, in moods both good and bad,
   we will find things in one another we do not like.
This is simply the way of life. But:
   To never hurt someone is to never love someone;
   to never be hurt is to never be loved.
   Why must the two go hand in hand?
Why do we bare our best and worst in the same place
   to the same person, though they may not deserve such extremes?
Maybe beings such as ourselves were not meant for close relationships;
   our intellect constantly battles with out instinct–
   what we feel tries to rule what we learn and know.
And yet we need each other–alone we merely exist, but together we can live!
Please try to see me as I am, soon you will know me better:
   my weaknesses, my trespasses, my idiosyncrasies, and bad habits.
It is so hard to change oneself, how can we hope to change another?
I have changed many things in many people,
   and seen them stay the same–yet not be the person I once knew.
This is one paradox of the human relationship.
We ask for change, demand it, then cannot accept it.
What do we want from one another?
If someone must change so for another, perhaps he or she has not really found
   a mate, or a friend, after all.
The struggle, the challenge, if you will, is to find something new and positive
   each day in someone that you love,
   and remain in touch with the way you feel about the negative and the familiar.
For these are the qualities ultimately most responsible for the fate of any
   relationship.
Do not run short of wonder and newness, don't fall into mundane patterns of life.
Renew each day who you are and what you feel, but retain the identity that is you.
You are the only person you can be, for yourself or anyone.
And if that should hurt you or someone you love, well . . . that's life!

Poems for the Head

Love Life
(In Memory of Alice Sabah)

You were always the one who embraced life,
Lived it to its fullest, never a moment wasted.
And I wondered, "What's the rush? There's so much time."
Time to do all the millions of things life has to offer.
Time to experience the joys of myriad performances,
To view those attractions both live and engrained on cellulose;
Time to try every dish ever cooked up by man.

But we just kid ourselves into thinking we'll get to it all.
There's just not time to do a fraction of all that waits.

You knew that, you took advantage of every waking moment.
You stretched yourself thin and grew fat on life.
Movies, shows, horse-pulls, outrageous media of all kinds—
The more bizarre, the better.
A smorgasbord of input, of experience, of life.
You lived, in the few years that I knew you,
More than many people do in a lifetime.
You seemed to have a firm grasp on your desire
to get in as much living as possible;
Knowing all too well how quickly life passes us by.

Without realizing it, you have taught me a great deal.
And yet, I've learned nothing.
Procrastinating my youth away, putting off life for a future time.
But there is no future. It belongs only to the billions yet unborn.
The present is all any of us ever have.
We steal the seconds, hoarding time against the end,
Only to have it slip through our clenched fingers.
Coldness and finality are the only certainties we can count on.
They are not something to look forward to.
And yet, they cannot be taken from us, nor given away.

Many wise people have contemplated the nature of life,
Each one reaching only the conclusions experience has
   shown them.
The realization of our hopes and dreams is beyond
   one lifetime.
Love and loss, joy and sorrow, life and death:
This is the nature of life.
Nothing can last because that is the law of the universe.
Galaxies and solar systems spin their way through frigid
   vacuum
To die eventually in the void of space,
None the wiser for their lengthy existence;
Powerless to maintain their place in this realm.

Surely we are greater than any celestial system,
blind and ignorant in the vastness of space.
We can look up on a clear night, reach out, and touch
   the heavens,
Nothing but thin air to separate us from the rest of
   the universe.

We are one with all we can see, touch, experience—
Part of a larger whole that we alone can perceive;
That only thinking, reasoning beings can appreciate.
A reality recognized by man; though we had no place in
   its creation.
We are impotent to change, to re-create, to re-direct the
   forces of existence.
We are bound to the great spheres of exploding plasma
   whirling through space
As surely as we are bound to the earth, and to one another.

New Dawn

The darkest night is roughly pierced
by the crown of a rising sun.
A new dawn breaks amazingly,
the darkness is undone.

Higher towards its zenith
the brilliant orb does climb;
Dawn grows into daylight
unclouded, clear this time.

A sky of blue highlighted
by dawn's receding gold,
Seems now to be near enough
to reach out for, and to hold.

The shadow demons grow shorter
(those vestiges of night)
Until they are all but lost
in the all-consuming light.

At last the sun peaks high above
directly overhead;
No coldness and no fear this time,
but warmth and strength instead.

The new day is upon us;
the night's become the past.
It seems certain that the daylight
is something that will last.

But now we see the yellow sphere
begin its slow decline;
Arcing towards the horizon,
diminishing its shine.

The orange glow of sunset
fades wearily from sight;
An all-encroaching darkness
ushers in the night.

Then blackness is upon us,
the candles we do burn;
Towards the waiting night-dreams
and somnolence we turn.

But sleep does not come easily,
dark memories remain.
Shadow-demons knock on the door
and on the window pane.

This time we ignore them
safe within our retreat;
We give up to unconsciousness
and float off into sleep.

We rest so very peacefully
and feel no loss or pain;
For now we know as sure as life
there'll be a new dawn again.

Versions

There are many ways to look inside,
to see into your soul;
To be as one in spirit and mind,
and make your being whole.

Some of us are quite in touch
we know our hopes and dreams;
Others go right through their lives,
and nothing is as it seems.

The routes we take are similar,
but no two paths are the same;
All the pieces on just one board,
yet we all play our own game.

We live, we love, we lose, we die,
that's what we all must do;
But how we deal with all life brings
makes me different from you.

Yet it seems we keep so much
hidden down below;
In a place beyond the outside's reach,
behind our outer glow.

They say to be in touch within
we must also seek without;
To join the inner and outer
is what the quest is all about.

We must keep an open mind,
and learn to try new things;
Seek out a new experience,
and the enlightenment it brings.

To understand life, we must live it,
observe as well as see;
To get what it is we want from life,
we must take it personally.

Yes, life comes in many versions,
some easy, some a heavy load;
We all must walk down different paths,
though we follow the same road.

IMPERATIVES

We must not slip into the mundanity of familiarity
when we have the capacity to make every day as if the first;
to find something new and fresh in everything we do.
We must never take one another for granted,
but savor the appreciation of favors small and large.
We must not forget the special feelings
we have for each other
that make solitude painful and distance unbearable.
We must not forsake one another, in action, deed, or word,
but keep true and open in all matters of head and heart.
We must not close our feelings off to ourselves and others,
be not blind to the undone or unspoken truths.
We must not forget the love and respect
we have for and give to one another.
We must not let go of one another.
We must not let go…
We must not…
We must…
We.

EMPTY WORDS

The world is full of empty words, we use them every day
We very often speak them when we've nothing else to say.
How do you do? The weather's fine! No one really shares.
The paper read…, The TV said…; Nobody really cares.
Poverty, war, abuse, crime, muggers, rapists, warmongers: slime!
We're just waiting for the bombs to fall–could happen any time.
There's terrorism in the USA; but we don't see it, no.
Can't miss our favorite sitcom, must catch our weekly show.
There's so much happening around us, yet few are at the wheel.
We live our lives, we work our jobs, distant from what we feel.
Some of us make a difference, most don't see the point.
Some do drugs, others drink, or smoke that daily joint.
In the end it doesn't matter, everyone must die.
We're so detached from our world, it makes the thinkers cry.
Apathy is killing us, no one escapes the blame
Some of us are activists, but most of us are too tame.
The things that really get to us, like taxes and parking fines,
Just don't seem to measure up to waterways set with mines.
And troops on alert or mobilized, ready to shoot and kill;
The missiles fly, the people die, the blood continues to spill.
Yet we just don't see it; can't happen here, we say
And we'll be blind and ignorant until that final day
When the radios and TVs blast warnings of our doom
We will just ignore them, feeling safe within our room;
And never know what hit us, yet we'll send those missiles back.
Or worse, we'll be the ones who initiate the attack.
The world will then be over–it cannot tolerate our wrath.
Eventually, though, life again will find a different path.
And grow it will–unchecked and free–as when it all began
Life can prosper wondrously, but not when "helped" by man.

Futility

How can I make it work?
Tediousness is the killer of your imagination,
the murderer of free thought.
Ah, free thought—the one thing impossible to put a price on.

My dreams, drowned out by the exhaustive repetition of
nonsensical humdrum which stifles my unconscious mind,
and limits my chance of escape.

To escape, mentally, for a time—to live my fantasies, secure in
the knowledge that their substanceless appeal will not hold me
bound to my deep desires and unperpetrated lusts.

I awaken now, unrested, surprised—the day is already upon me.
There are no excuses to hold me at home, only reasons to get
out and make my way.

Real rest is in the dreams that let you leave your usual
surroundings for a distant land of fulfilled pleasures and
unrestricted play—a playground of the mind, if you will.

Will—that which makes us live, no matter how tough or
oppressive life becomes; that which enables man to reach far
beyond his limited physical scope to attain the very heavens.

Heaven is not just a place we go when we die (usually we go
into a box underground).
It is a realm we must create now, on earth, while we are alive.
Only during life can we enjoy that which it imparts to us—a
feeling of wholeness, of being a part of the vast collection of
physical matter that makes up our universe.

Our universe? Surely we are not alone in such a unimaginably
vast space of reality.
Our neighbors, although we haven't met them, are out there,
somewhere. Perhaps they watch and wait; maybe they are wise
and have learned eternal patience. They are waiting to teach us.

But why must they wait? I want my children to know a world that
knows itself—its potential and its failures. . .but mostly its capacity
to love and be loved.

Night
Light

Night closes in like an angry fist
    tight with hatred about a fragile limb.
Storms with eyes of fury batter like incessant
    waves on a craggy, jagged reef.
Darkness is a coffin lid, shut tight against eternity.
    And yet there is light within.
A tiny glow flickers timidly in damp, dusty caverns
    of thought.
So little illumination for so vast a reality,
    if indeed this be.
A mere flame to guide us through a universe
    of blackness.
It is not quite sufficient, but it is all we have.
Therefore, we make use of its gift.
We go gently, so as not to extinguish its source—
    the hopes and dreams of its bearers.
As we move forward, it grows ever so slightly.
Hopeful, we feed it with our love, shield it from
    our fears, and from hate.
Stronger, the light becomes a shaft,
    then a wide beam pointing the way;
    a vanguard against the emptiness.
Now we can see where we are going,
    but not what will happen when we get there.

Present Past

Life was so easy when I was young,
I hadn't a care in the world.
Things came so easy—just asked and got,
my troubles had not yet unfurled.

As I got older, things got more complex,
my thoughts moved from candy to money.
Fight for your place lest you fall underfoot,
what happened to all that was funny?

The days they came, the days they went,
and when they are gone, they're forgotten.
Memories are just ephemeral things
like fruit off the vine that grows rotten.

So I packed them away in boxes and crates,
and stored them all up in the attic.
The bad ones remain and the good fade away,
it seems to be all automatic.

When you look at your life and try to go back,
it's never as you did remember.
Memories, like fires, will soon die away
Leaving naught but a glowing ember.

And soon, that too will douse and die,
the past melted into a dream.
It slips from your mind like the tide from a beach,
and things were just not as they seem.

The friends I had, both good and bad,
I let them all slip away.
New ones I make are neither better or worse,
Yet I find that they, too do not stay.

Now in my life are so many new things,
I just don't have time for the past.
Cause when it's the present, it's "here to stay,"
We forget that nothing can last.

PERPETUAL . . .

Unlike fluid, flowing time
   drifting in random direction;
my life is in stasis, it does not move,
   perhaps this is my intention.

I see all around me sad people,
   their woes;
they carry them like an affliction.
They struggle with demons within
   and without,
their misery becomes an addiction.

And here I sit, beyond it all,
watching passively as life goes by.
They water their lives with floods of
   tears,
while mine, stagnated, grows dry.

I feel no hurt, no pain, nor loss;
completely detached from life.
I drift through its various incidents
totally devoid of strife.

Maybe I am too separate
from that which makes living real;
Ignorant of my complexities,
out of touch with the way I feel.

In the course of my life
   these feelings change.
It's so hard to keep track
   of things long range.

Events rule my thoughts
   as the queen rules the hive.
No will of my own
   save the need to survive.

But living is more than maintaining
   vital biological functions:
It's growing and learning how to cope
   in all of life's critical junctions.

It's facing your problems one at
   a time
and finding for each a solution.
It's caring, sharing, and trying
   to make
a valuable contribution.

These words I preach, they sound
   so quaint,
yet they're all just empty chatter;
A fine philosophy, if you please,
but to me it just doesn't matter.

Nothing I do is exciting,
my life is so uninviting.
I'd like to do something delighting,
but I guess I'll just stick to writing.

Father and Son and Father

A father wanted to talk to his son,
but the baby had not yet been born.
"I'll have to wait till he's here," he said,
feeling very forlorn.

A father wanted to talk to his son,
but the infant was not even one.
"I guess I'll wait til he grows some more,
at his age it wouldn't be fun."

A father wanted to talk to his son,
since his child had just turned three.
"I really should wait til he's bigger;
he wouldn't understand me."

A father wanted to talk to his son,
now that the boy was six.
"I guess I'll give him a little more time,
so everything I tell him sticks."

A father wanted to talk to his son,
Though the youngster was nearly ten.
"I think I'll wait til he's older," he thought,
"we'll have the chance again."

A father wanted to talk to his son,
but the man fell ill and died.
The son is nearly grown and thinks
his father never tried.

A father wanted to talk to his son,
but the two of them just never shared.
Now the son is a father himself
and he knows that his dad really cared.

Why can't I seem to write anymore?
The words just slip away.
I put my pen to the paper
and don't know what to say.

I've got so many feelings inside
I want to articulate
But when I try to write them down
my mind won't let me create.

I want to forge a separate world
formed from my hopes and dreams;
Express my wonderment at life,
review my plans and schemes.

Build a realm of imagining
where all my thoughts run free;
Examine the range of emotions
from joy to misery.

And yet I keep me locked up tight,
these things I cannot share.
The illusion of understanding
becomes a mental snare.

It snatches at my sanity
Tries to drag me under.
And though I strive for clarity
It rips my mind asunder.

The pieces, once fragmented,
Drift purposelessly apart.
I cannot draw them together,
There is no place to start.

Entropy takes hold of me
my consciousness does drift
into the yawning blackness
of a dark, eternal rift.

A place from which I can't escape,
a void bereft of hope.
Where there is such screaming
   loneliness
The human mind can't cope.

And so into itself it shrinks,
a black hole of the soul.
There is no coming back again,
if reality be the goal.

So do not lose track of your
   thoughts;
they are the essence of you.
Remember them, and write them
   down,
and to yourself always be true.

The Magic Crystal

My life was at its lowest ebb
when I walked up to the store.
The sign read "Gallery of Minerals,"
and I stepped on through the door.

The place was filled with treasures:
carved ivory and totem poles,
Wooden ships in bottles,
and soapstone trays and bowls.

There was coral laid on a table,
Antique weapons hung on a wall.
If I spent a lifetime here,
I couldn't see it all.

Then I turned a corner
and saw, to my surprise,
A showcase full of jewelry
of every shape and size.

Some was made of mother-of-pearl,
some was made from bones.
There were lustrous metals
and semi-precious stones.

The riches of the earth were here
all taken from nature's hand.
Gifts of men and animals
From the sea and from the land.

Then in a special section
over in the back,
Was a showcase full of minerals—
I was on the right track.

I stepped up to the counter,
and stared at the display.
The crystals were hypnotic,
I could not look away.

Some were set in silver,
others set in gold.
But all of them were beautiful
Exquisite to behold.

They all appeared to be perfect,
I couldn't make a choice.
Then one seemed to call to me
as if it had a voice.

The salesman gave it to me,
I held it in my grasp.
I reached up to my silver chain
and opened up the clasp.

As soon as it was on me
I felt my energy change.
I knew my life from this point on
would never be the same.

I still wear that crystal,
together we do grow.
And where my life is going
neither of us can know.

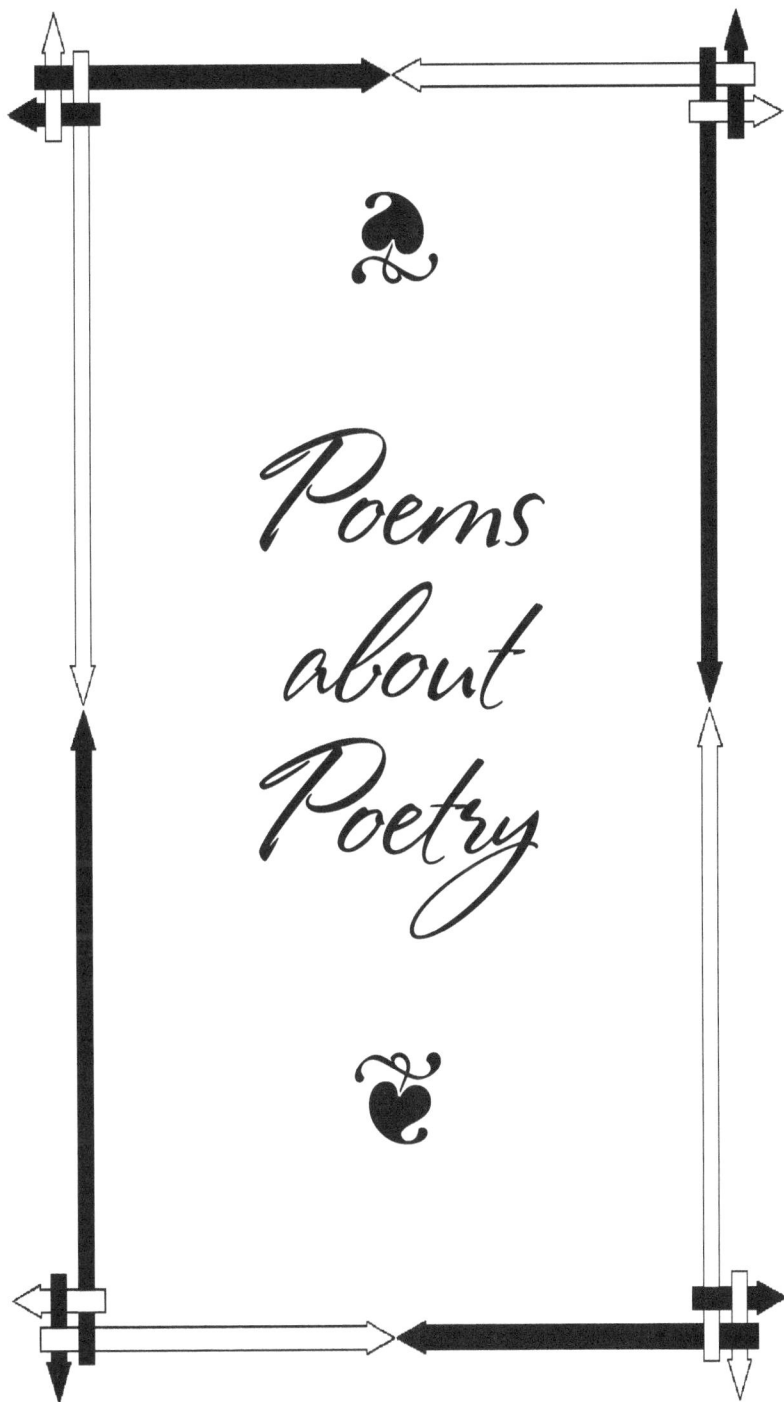

Poems about Poetry

FROST IN THE CITY

Whose streets these are I do not know;
I'm walking in the Village, though.
No one notices me stopping here
to watch the streets pile up with snow.

A homeless man must think me queer
to stop without some shelter near.
My frozen fingers begin to ache,
On the coldest evening of the year.

He gives my jacket sleeve a shake
to ask if there's some change to take.
The only other noise is the beep
of cars as they proceed, then brake.

The snow is lovely, white and deep;
but I have appointments to keep.
And blocks to go before I sleep.
And blocks to go before I sleep.

The Creative Edge

You think your creative edge is gone
Baby, that's just not so.
Your talents, gifts, and excellence
are hidden down below.

Covered by doubts,
buried by fears;
faced with uncertainty,
washed with tears.

Cast aside this awful stone
that grinds away your edge;
Raise it up and make it whole
and to yourself do pledge:

My life is mine and mine alone,
but my gifts belong to all.
My mission here is to share them
with one and all the world.

Origins

The words come to my tongue;
where do they come from?

Heart and head in the same place;
yet separate.

Feelings formed of similar thoughts;
though conflicting.

Emotions brought forth from
unconscious conclusions;
but struggling.

Life created through a spark of love;
alas, warring.

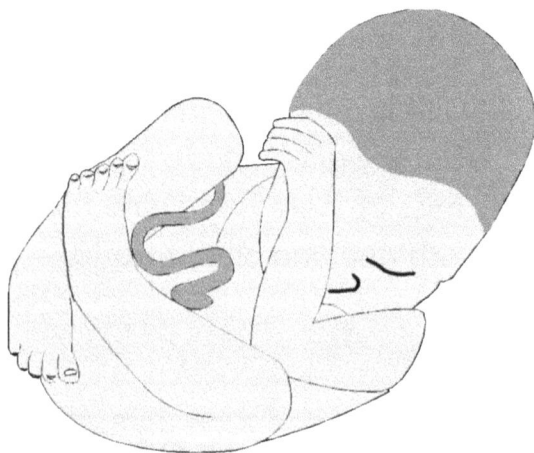

MONO LOGUE

It isn't every day I feel the need or urge to write.
Sometimes words flow trippingly, sometimes they
  are tight.

Often, need forced hand to pen, stylus placed on paper;
Ideas that grow inspired-like, other times do taper.

Concentration is the key—to focus on an idea,
If my inner thoughts shout loud enough, my
  consciousness will hear.

I must keep my inner ear tuned to what I think,
So I'll know when I'm ready—when I'm on the brink:

Then out will rush these buried thoughts from their
  hiding place,
To make their mark upon the page, across its
  blue-ruled face.

There's so much that needs to be said, so much that's
  good and true,
So many things that must be heard, by me and also
  by you.

Yes, I could go the rest of my days without ere lifting
  a pen,
But if I betrayed my inner voice, where would I be then?

A stifled man, a choking soul—strangled from within,
to lock my feelings deep inside would be a mortal sin.

So once again I lift my pen and place it on the page,
My quill becomes an actor upon a paper stage.

Free Verse (Cause I'll Never Be Able to SELL It)

This here poem has no rhyme scheme
so don't expect it to rhyme.
The rhythm's there and so is the meter,
but don't get your hopes up high.

Just because a word is placed
far at the end of a line.
Doesn't mean that the word underneath
Has to sound alike.

Sounds are simple, words are easy;
it's language that's a bind.
Sometimes it's hard enough just to write
without attempting a rhyme.

Now let's talk about grasshoppers' knees
(I didn't even know they had them).
I've never seen someone quite that short.
(If I have it wasn't that often).

Let's discuss some "old wive's tails"
(I didn't even know they had them).
Do they grow cause they're old or cause they're wed?
(Or do they grow because of the husband?)

That last verse was silly, unnecessarily so,
but I couldn't help it a bit.
I always speak out when I think of a pun;
sometimes I should just bite my lip.

I'm trying to find out what life is about
to date I don't think it's been done.
But I'll have fun as I make the attempt
cause I can't try after I'm gone.

It's odd to think I'd be here no more
to work, to struggle, to survive.
But it's nice to think I did all that I could
to put up a pretty good fight.

Rhyming Poem (As Opposed to Free Verse)

This is a poem of an interesting kind,
It's specially metered and carefully lined.
Each word has a rhythm all its own
and like ancient drums beat with a bone
tells us a story of this world's plight
and brings our problems into the light.

Poems let us see our inner self
(long forgotten, gathering dust on a shelf).
If we can show, on paper, what's trapped inside,
If we verbalize the feelings too many of us hide,
Then we would see that we're really the same:
We live, we die—we all play the game.

Some play by the rules, others don't;
  Some help one another, others won't.
Some people complain, and some people rant;
  Some people love, but many just can't.
Some people work, some people fight;
  Many are wrong, though most think they're right.

But we are still human—our most common tie;
we live out our lives; at the end we die.
Time isn't physical, yet it binds us as such,
Time is all around us, but we don't get too much.
The short time we have is precious indeed,
one thing we find: it's more time that we need.

Time to cry and time to lose,
  time to laugh and joke and muse.
Time to wonder or be afraid,
  time to get shafted, time to get paid.
Time to find out what everything means,
  (why some wear suits and some wear jeans).
Time to run and time to crawl,
  time to do everything or nothing at all.

We must take life one step at a time;
Take all the words and make our poetry rhyme.

Purpose

They say that poems should come from the heart
But I don't think that's true.
The best of poems come straight from the head
and here's what they should do:

Take you oh so far away
to a place where you've never been,
and show you sights of wonderment—
Things you've never seen.
But a poem can seem a darker place
Of hurt, despair, and strife;
A world of desperate loneliness—
A thing that we call life.

But to each coin there's another side
we cannot see for the first.
A poem's job is to make illusions real
and stir within us such thirst
That we will plunge into the void
headlong, without delay;
And swim among the wordless thoughts
and sounds it does not say.

Dive into its mysteries
and with its message play
For you may not understand it all
until some later day.

And there you be, just standing there
with head held loose in hand,
and it will strike you all at once
Though it was never planned.
Then you will see the author's end
as surely as your own—
The poet's life is the same as yours:
We live—and die—alone.

Poems for Fun

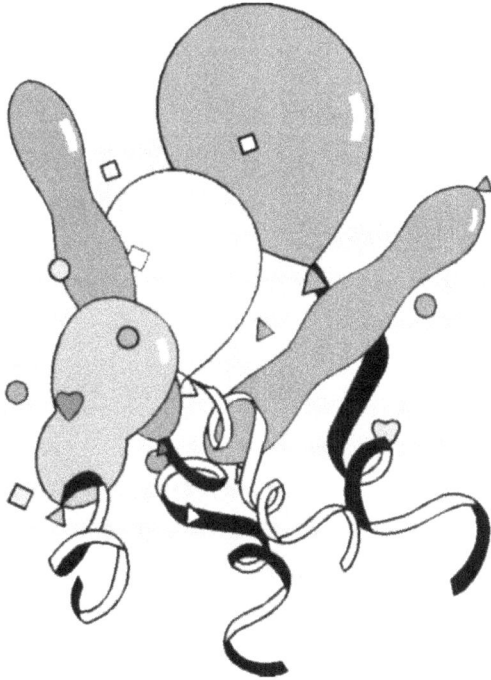

Home Grown

Poems are silly,
poems are fun.
Poems are over
when they are done.
Start to write and follow your pen,
lift it up when you get to the end.
Read it over and check each line,
but don't change a thing—
it sounds just fine.

Sit you down and write one more,
if not at a desk then on the floor.
Don't think hard, just write what you feel,
but never copy and never steal.
The poem you write must be your own;
the best of them are always home grown.

My Life, My Umbrella

I take it with me wherever I go,
  don't like to get caught in the rain.
Closed it's a weapon to protect
  and defend,
Open, it covers my brain.

Else the water would run right in
  and make an awful flood;
My head would turn to soggy mush,
  my brain would turn into mud.

Then out my ears, a quick egress,
  my thoughts, my feelings and all.
Then I'd start writing poetry
  that was completely off the wall.

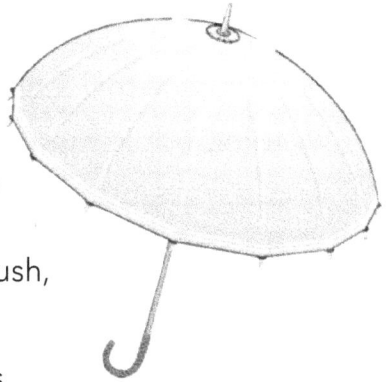

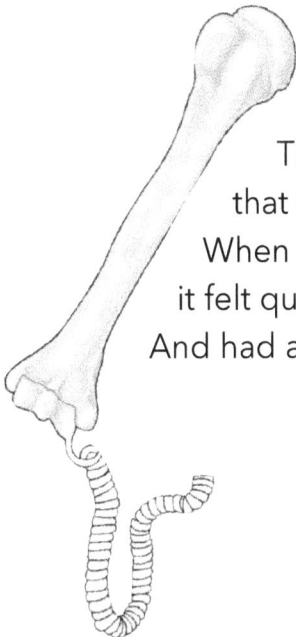

There once was a telephone,
  that was made in the shape of a bone.
  When held to ear
  it felt quite queer;
And had a strange dial tone.

Come to me with your dreams so sweet
Touch me softly as I sleep.
Leave me with a dream so fine
Of another place and time.
Take me oh so far away
To a special magical place
Where people meet and fall in love
and it's not just something we're
    dreaming of.

Bad Air

Mr. Atmosphere is our friend;
though he is nearly at the end.

He no longer stops those awful rays,
pollutants have got him in a haze.

So if you sit out in the sun
put on lots of stuff.

Mr. Atmosphere is growing weak
and Mr. Sun is tough!

TAROT

Everything you touch
and everything that touches you
has meaning.

But everything depends on
your interpretation of
what was, what is,
and what will be.

These are the three states
of reality.

As we pass through them,
they are in constant change;

And yet, they remain
the same.

Model's Lament

Do you realize how beautiful you are?
Do you realize that men, from afar,
come closer to see
your dazzling beauty?

Have you heard it all before?
Has it been spoken as a man holds the door
to let you pass
while he watches your ass?

Are you avoided, too lovely to behold
Or around you do men become so bold
that they won't hesitate
to ask you for a date?

What is it like to feel people stare?
Is it appreciated, or do you not even care
as they pass you by
and let out a sigh?

Or do you think there are some who fear,
And become undone whenever you're near?
A lethal dose
If one comes too close!

Ah, if all of us were so aesthetically pleasing;
if we all were as pretty as flowers in season . . .
Then talk of beauty would be just empty wording,
and you would not carry your lovely burden.

SMOKER'S LAMENT

My lungs are filled with
    blackened soot,
they scarcely can draw air,
Looking at my X-rays
is more than I can bear.

I wheeze, I hack and sputter,
the smoke makes me real sick.
I really don't want another
deadly cancer-stick.

My breath smells like an
    ashtray,
My teeth are yellowish brown.
So I never even smile,
just wear this dreadful frown.

I feel that I am killing myself,
sucking down this smoke.
But I'll still have another one
though I feel like I will choke.

I cannot smell the flowers,
I cannot taste my food.
I can't enjoy my lover's kiss
(although I'm sure it's good).

I really must do something
to end this dependence fast.
If I can't stop this addiction
I'm just not going to last.

It really isn't funny,
the problem's quite severe.
I think if I don't stop real soon,
I'll die within the year.

So the next time that I feel I need
to light a cigarette,
I'll read this little warning
and try hard to forget . . .

This thing that has control
    over me,
and robs me of my breath.
Cause I know for a certainty
it's sure to cause my death.

And when they cut me open
to see what was the cause,
a plume of viscous smoke will
    rise
and bear its cancerous claws.

Chaucer Adored Women so Much...

(Some thoughts after reading Chaucer's *The Wife of Bath*)

I'm a professor from Stony Brook
and I love the way the students look
up to me to learn the truth
And so I teach them Chaucer, for sooth.
I tell them it's nothing, it's easy, you see.
But I know reading Old English takes an eternity
of time they don't have, until the exam
when into their aching brains they must cram
this ludicrousness of the wife of Bath
who screwed up her husbands and had the last laugh.
and planned and plotted each lecherous deed
until a new husband she happened to need.
To steal his money, his faith, and his life
and constantly nag him and cause him such strife
That he had to flee this reality.
Can such things as I teach them possibly be?
So if you don't think Chaucer liked women,
read some of his work, I think it's a given.
From his viewpoint and directness of stand,
I'd say he thought women were too out of hand,
and had to be taught to behave and obey
or they would just lie around and have sex all day.
I don't think it's sexist, but I don't think it's fair
to turn women into spiders who trap men in their lair,
and wrap them with troubles spun from within,
suck out their life and leave them so thin
that they run for a cover, a cover of earth;
for death is really just the flip side of birth!

It takes a mind by woman spurned,
one that's been so badly burned
to write such cutting poetry
because of some uptight lady
who wouldn't give him all that she had
for whatever reasons, good or bad.
A man named Freud later defined
that term as "psychotic jealousy" (before he pined)
and died of something called lack of sex,
(a thing for which men have broken their necks).
It seems that Chaucer had this problem serious,
from women he just seemed to obtain a weariness
of body and mind no spirits could lift
even though women claim to have the gift
of joy and beauty and charm and love.
I don't believe he got nearly enough.
Maybe the women he knew were no good;
Although out of so many you'd think that he could
find a girl who didn't scheme and plot and lie,
and make his life so miserable he wanted to die.
But alas our pal led a lonely life—
someone like him could not stand a wife
to chide him on faults he could not have conceived
of terrible treasons not to be believed.
Of all things that men are infamous for:
lying and cheating and stealing, and more.
Yes, this is the price you pay when you wed.
In Chaucer's opinion, you're better off dead.
So if you'd ask me that question again
I'd answer that Chaucer had a fancy for men.

About the Author

GARY A. ROSENBERG is a graphic artist and typesetter living in South Florida with his editor wife and a houseful of animals. Together, Gary & Carol are The Book Couple, specializing in helping authors self-publish their books in the traditional style.

Most of these poems were written in the turbulent months following the downfall of Gary's first marriage and his fortuitous meeting with Carol on a crowded train platform in New York City.